T4-ALI-581

You Will Find
the Right Person
for Your Family's Needs . . .

if you ask the right questions! Here are some vital examples:

- Are you working now—how long have you been there?
- How many children are you taking care of—how old are they?
- Can you cook? Drive?
- Will you work overtime?
- Do you smoke?
- Will you take care of pets?
- Do you have references I can check in advance of an interview?

Picking the Perfect Nanny guides you every step of the way!

_____

About the author: Jane P. Metzroth is Vice President and Director of Human Resources for a major corporation headquartered in New York City. She is also the mother of two children and the employer of a perfect nanny. She has assisted many professionals, in particular first-time parents, in finding quality childcare for their families.

Picking The Perfect Nanny:

A Foolproof Guide to the Best At-Home Childcare

by Jane P. Metzroth

PUBLISHED BY POCKET BOOKS NEW YORK

POCKET BOOKS, a division of Simon & Schuster, Inc.,
1230 Avenue of the Americas, New York, N.Y. 10020

Copyright © 1984, 1986 by Jane P. Metzroth
Illustrations © 1984 by Debbie Insetta
Cover artwork copyright © 1986 by Fredericka Ribes

Published by arrangement with the author

ISBN: 0-671-62627-2

First Pocket Books trade paperback printing July, 1986

10 9 8 7 6 5 4 3 2 1

POCKET and colophon are registered trademarks
of Simon & Schuster, Inc.

Printed in the U.S.A.

To Dorothy
With Special Thanks For The Loving Care
You Have Given
Erik and Alexander

With appreciation to the
production coordinator, Ginger Rice,
for all of her effort

CONTENTS

Picking The Perfect Nanny

INTRODUCTION

Picking the Perfect Nanny: A Foolproof Guide to the Best At-Home Child-care is designed to assist the career mother, father or couple in selecting *permanent* home childcare. It is written for the professional parent interested in refining the process of picking the best childcare *on the first try.*

This book will be invaluable to you if you are:

- a pregnant woman who wants to return to her career immediately but does not know how to begin to find good childcare,

- a mother who is contemplating the return to her career after a hiatus,

- a single parent (male or female) who must suddenly return to the job market,

- a single father, who because of divorce or death of a spouse, needs qualified childcare immediately,

- a working couple who has gone through a series of housekeepers and swears that no good childcare exists.

HAPPY READING

BACKGROUND

In 1976, when I was pregnant with my first child, finding good childcare was not an easy project. I listened to a few women who were working mothers, but most of their stories centered around the negative quality of childcare available to a career couple. So, when my son was born, I was basically "on my own" to find quality care.

I began by contacting an employment agency that I had read about in a local newspaper and was naive enough to ask the agency to set up applicant appointments in their office. I envisioned an organized setting with scheduled applicants waiting to be interviewed for my position. When I arrived at this agency, I was confronted, instead, with a large waiting room full of men and women, all unemployed, and all looking for jobs. None of them were there specifically with me in mind, and the owners of the agency informed me that I was welcome to interview anyone or everyone in the room until I found someone suitable. Thinking that this must be the standard way it was done, I proceeded to interview everyone in the room. I found a woman who seemed to be competent, because she told me she had worked as a kindergarten teacher in her native country. Taking the references that she provided, I went home and phoned everyone on the list. I discovered that there seemed to be a common thread linking all the references. In fact, they all sounded as if they were related to the applicant. Since I had nowhere else to turn, at least that is what I thought at the time, I hired this woman as a live-in housekeeper. *Luckily* for me, the situation turned out to be successful. She was with us for 18 months, but when we moved out of state, she did not want to come along.

At that time, I again faced the ordeal of looking for another housekeeper to take care of my son. The second time around I was a little bit smarter but still had not really developed an organized approach to finding good home childcare. I contacted two employment agencies and asked both of them to send candidates to my home, as opposed to going into the agencies for another "cattle call". I had at least a dozen people arrive at my home over a two day period, and from this group, I picked a woman who seemed to be right for our family. I received her list of references and called all of them. I interviewed the references over the phone, in more detail than I had with the first housekeeper, and when I was satisfied that the past references seemed to be legitimate, I made an employment offer for a live-out position. This woman stayed with us for approximately two years, but she was eventually fired for chronic lateness. The lateness problem was really there from the start, but being reluctant to face the problem, I lived with it. Every morning, I also lived with the fear that she would either be late, therefore I would be late for work, or not come at all.

It was time to hire housekeeper number three. Several weeks prior to firing the second housekeeper, I decided that I should develop a strategy to successfully pick the third housekeeper. Then, I would not have to go through sleepless nights worrying whether or not my child was well taken care of, whether the housekeeper was going to come to work, whether the housekeeper was going to be late, whether the housekeeper was going to quit — all of the things that go through working parents' minds if they are not convinced that the person who is taking care of their child or children and their home is the right person in the first place.

In my line of work, I interview people on a daily basis for employment with the company. There are ways to pre-screen, interview, and select people that can reduce the odds of a "bad pick". Since the technique that I used at work was successful, I felt that if I employed the same technique in picking housekeepers, I could reduce my chances of making a "bad pick" for my home.

The contents of this book were developed in 1980 to deal effectively with the problem of finding my third housekeeper. I can happily say that the hours spent in developing the technique proved to be successful. The same woman has been taking care of my son for the past six years. Because she has been excellent in all phases of childcare and in caring for my home, I no longer live in fear that when I wake up and get ready to go to work, my housekeeper will not be in my home taking care of my family which has now increased in size to two children. I can, with assurance, tell you that employing the methods outlined in the rest of this book will give you a much better opportunity of finding someone to properly care for your child and your home on a long term basis. It will also spare you the agony which most of us have experienced when confronted with the possibility that the housekeeper who you have selected will end up being replaced many times over.

Chapter I

How to **Know** What You Need

HOW TO KNOW WHAT YOU NEED

You know you need to find quality childcare for your home. You also know that it would be great to find a caring person who would look after the housekeeping. That is usually the extent of what most of us know when we approach the problem of finding a housekeeper/nanny. What you need to know, however, is the complete description of the job you want done BEFORE you bring someone in to do it.

When I recruit personnel for my employer, I develop a thorough written job description by talking at length with the manager of the area with the opening. I am interested in finding out about a typical day, but more importantly, an atypical one. The "out of the ordinary" day is the one that could make the previously uninformed or unwarned employee quit.

The same idea holds true for your home. You need to talk at length with your spouse (if you have one) and, silly as it may seem, with yourself. The questionnaire which follows is designed to make you really think about your child(ren), your home, and your career. Fill it out HONESTLY (even the questions that seem unimportant)! Your answers will be used as the framework for selecting the right person for your family.

Family Fact Sheet

I. CHILD(REN)

  A.   **AGE**   **SEX**

    1.

    2.

    3.

    4.

  B. If your child(ren) is over age 5 what are his/her after school activities:

    1. List all sports, clubs, hobbies, religious instruction, friends, etc.

    2. How many of these require transportation?

  C. What does your child(ren) do during school breaks? [Christmas and Easter, winter break/spring break]

  D. What does your child(ren) do on school holidays or one day closings?

E. What does your child(ren) do during summer vacation?

   1. No Camp
   2. Day Camp
   3. Sleep Away Camp

F. If your child(ren) is between the ages of 2 and 5 does (s)he attend nursery school or a play group?

   1. How many days per week?
   2. Is transportation required?
   3. Must the child(ren) bring lunch?

G. If your child(ren) does not attend school what do you want him or her to do all day?

   1. Go to a playground or park
   2. Play in your yard
   3. Play indoors
   4. Watch children's programs on television
   5. Other

H. What time does your child(ren) get up in the morning and go to bed in the evening? Does (s)he take a nap?

I. Who will bring your child(ren) to the doctor and dentist for routine check-ups?

   1. Is transportation required?

J. What do you feed your child(ren) for breakfast, lunch and dinner?

   1. Does (s)he eat snacks?
   2. Do you allow "junk food"?
   3. What does (s)he refuse to eat ?

II. THE HOUSE/APARTMENT

A. Lay-Out

1. Number of rooms
2. Number of bathrooms
3. Is there a playroom for the child(ren)?
4. Is there more than one floor?
5. Is there a separate room with bath for live-in help?

B. Which of the following appliances do you have?

1. Washing Machine
2. Dryer
3. Dishwasher
4. Microwave Oven
5. Vacuum Cleaner/Carpet Sweeper
6. Self cleaning or conventional oven

C. How many loads of wash do you do each week?

1. Do you want ironing done?
2. Does eveything go in the dryer?
3. Do shirts go to an outside laundry [if so, does the laundry pick-up and deliver]?

D. How many times per week do you shop for groceries?

1. Is the grocery store within walking distance?
2. Does the grocery store deliver?

E. Who does the heavy housekeeping?

1. Window washing
2. Rug shampooing
3. Floor waxing
4. "Spring Cleaning"

F. Do you have pets?

1. Who feeds, walks and bathes them?

III. YOU [AND YOUR SPOUSE IF APPLICABLE]

A. What time do you leave for work?

1. Do you like to make breakfast for your child(ren) before you go?

B. What time do you arrive home?

1. Do you like to eat dinner with your child(ren)?

C. How many times each week do you need to stay late in your office?

1. What time do you arrive home?

D. How far is your office from home?

1. How long does it take you to commute during rush-hour?
2. How long would it take you to get home at an off-hour if you had an emergency?

Chapter II
How to **Find** What You Need

HOW TO FIND WHAT YOU NEED

Whether you are currently pregnant and anticipate finding your first housekeeper, or if you have gone through a series of housekeepers and are at your wits-end about where to find the next one, you need to know that there are more available sources for finding good childcare for your home than using employment agencies. This is not to say that using an employment agency is necessarily the wrong approach. As a matter of fact, many fine housekeepers have been found from this valuable resource. I will be covering the best ways to pick and work with an agency in your area later in this chapter. I am going to begin by giving you a list of other sources of good, but not necessarily expensive, childcare.

Using Your Local Newpaper

Most newspapers have a classified section entitled "Situation Wanted" where people looking for employment will advertise their qualifications. Go through the column carefully and pick those advertisements that come closest to what you are looking for in childcare for your home.

Placing Your Own Advertisement

This method has an associated expense. Most newpapers charge a modest fee to run a classified advertisement either in the Sunday paper or, in some cases, in the daily paper with the option to use the Sunday supplement for an additional advertisement. Take advantage of that option. It is important to run your advertisement in a Sunday paper because that is when most people have enough time to spend reading the classified section. When you write your advertisement, pattern it after an advertisement that you have seen in the local paper, and make sure that you put in the details that are important to the way you want things done. For example, if you want someone in your home between the hours of 8:00 a.m. and 6:00 p.m., make sure you specify that in your ad. If you do not, you will get responses from people who will not be able to be in your home at 8:00 a.m. or stay in your home until 6:00 p.m. This method of being specific on the important details will save you needless time on the phone responding to people who have no semblance of being right for the job that you want done.

When I have helped friends place ads for help in local newspapers, I advise them to put a telephone number, rather than a post office box, for response. Most people who are looking for work as housekeepers or nannies are not going to sit down and write you a letter explaining their qualifications, nor do the majority of them have a resume'. Therefore, for the most responses, it is much easier to provide a phone number for interested housekeepers to call. Now obviously, if you get a big response, you will be spending the better part of the week that follows the running of your advertisement answering your telephone. I have found that either purchasing an answering machine or borrowing an answering machine from a friend and attaching it to your home telephone during the week that the advertisement runs can save you many "ups and downs" and wasted time on the telephone. Put a short message on the answering machine that says that you are unable to come to the phone. The caller should leave a telephone number and a message and you will phone back. At the end of every day, collect the messages and phone the people that you feel "sounded right" to you over the telephone. From that group, you should be able to find several viable candidates for interviews.

I have included several examples of well-constructed newspaper advertisements below.

These sample advertisements will narrow your applicant pool considerably. The more specific you can be where it is necessary, the closer you will come to the perfect pick on the first try. Obviously, in order to save money on your advertisement, use abbreviations and drop unnecessary words where possible.

EXAMPLES OF NEWSPAPER ADVERTISEMENTS

I. Childcare with Housekeeping (Live-Out)

HOUSEKEEPER (Can Substitute NANNY, GOVERNESS, CHILDCARE MONITOR)

To take charge of 2 girls, ages 9 and 2. Additional duties include cooking for children, laundry and light housekeeping in a 10 room home. Live-out Mon-Fri 8:00 a.m. to 6:00 p.m. with flexibility for overtime. Driver's license required. References will be checked. Call Jane, weekdays after 7:00 p.m. (212) 555-1234.

II. Childcare without Housekeeping (Live-Out)

NANNY (Can Substitute HOUSEKEEPER, GOVERNESS, CHILDCARE MONITOR)

Single Parent needs caring person to live-out and take charge of 2 children, boy age 9 and girl age 2. Arrange after school play dates for boy, spend time outdoors with girl. Must have drivers license and recent checkable references. Monday-Friday 8:00 a.m. to 6:00 p.m. Must be flexible and non-smoker. Call Jane after 7:00 p.m. (212) 555-1234.

III. Childcare with Housekeeping (Live-In)

HOUSEKEEPER (Can Substitute NANNY, GOVER-NESS, CHILDCARE MONITOR)

Two-career couple needs caring person to live-in and take charge of two children and 10 room home located 30 minutes from New York City. Duties include cooking for 2 boys ages 9 and 2, laundry, grocery shopping and light housekeeping. Must have driver's license and checkable references. 5½ day week; 8:00 a.m. to 6:00 p.m. Monday-Friday plus every other Saturday. Own room and bath with private entrance. Call Jane, weekdays after 7:00 p.m. (212) 555-1234.

Here are some points worth noting:

- It is important to clearly state the age(s) of your child(ren) and, if you think it is relevant, the sex. The reader who does not like to care for children under age 5 or prefers to take care of girls, when you have boys, will be tipped off before wasting everyone's time on the phone.

- The live-in housekeeper should know how far you are from a major town or city for planning her weekend travel. You should also detail the living arrangements as clearly as possible. If she has to share a room with your child, make sure you indicate that in your advertisement. Those who do not like that arrangement will not bother calling you.

- In all examples, the work week is clearly defined, but a qualifier for overtime flexibility has been added for the live-out position. If things like smoking (or non-smoking) or a driver's license are important to you, make sure to incorporate them into your advertisement.

- Confine call-backs to a specific time of the day. Although you may have an answering machine picking up the calls, it keeps the ringing to a prescribed period, and if you feel like picking up the phone, you know you will be there.

- Never give your last name. You do not want unhappy candidates to know who you are or to be able to know where you live.

- Finally, you should never talk about a salary in the advertisement. If you don't know how to price the job, you are safer leaving the salary out to avoid turning off good candidates by going too low. Conversely, you do not need to "give away the store" by committing to a salary in print if the market is lower. The time to talk money is when someone who meets your requirements has been searched out.

Before I leave the topic of newspaper advertisements, let me suggest one other source for your advertisement. In major cities across the country, you can run your advertisement in foreign newspapers. Many times, people who are entering this country and looking for work are more apt to pick up a newspaper from their own country rather than one from your city.

Sources At The Work Place

As a working parent, there are many resources at your office which you can utilize to find quality childcare. For example, if there is a bulletin board where general information can be posted, check the board to see if anyone has placed an advertisement because their housekeeper is going to be available. If there are no advertisements on the board for housekeepers, put one of your own on the bulletin board, once again explaining your requirements in some detail and the hours that you are looking for help at home. If your company has a corporate newspaper or newsletter, place an advertisement in that resource.

Womens'and/or Parents' Groups

Check your area for working womens' or working parents' organizations. One of the topics that always comes up at these sessions is where to find good housekeepers. The more contacts you have with other working parents, the greater your network of housekeeper resources is going to be.

If you cannot find a working womens' or parents' organization in your area, create one of your own. Run a small advertisement in a local newspaper inviting working parents to join you in your home for coffee at a specified date and time, preferably after the work day is over. Make the topic for your first meeting "Finding Good Childcare in the Home." You will be surprised how much each working parent knows about the subject.

The Doctor's Office

While waiting in the Obstetrician's or Pediatrician's office, ask the people who are sitting around you if they found good childcare and where they found it. Don't be shy about bringing up the subject. Once again, when asked, parents will quickly volunteer the good and the bad stories about finding childcare for their home. Listen to where they have and have not been successful in getting this childcare and eliminate the unsuccessful sources from your list of resources.

The Schools

If you have a private school in the area that you live, visit the school, because many of them have bulletin boards that are full of notices and advertisements posted by housekeepers looking for work. Place an ad on the bulletin board at a local university and you may be able to attract a student who will exchange childcare duties for room and board. Also, if you are the parent of a school age child, ask your child's teacher for the names of working mothers in your child's class. Contact those mothers and find out if they know where good childcare is available.

Nanny Training Schools

If your needs do not include housekeeping, an excellent source of childcare can be found in the graduating class of a nanny training school. Located throughout the country, these schools usually recruit students with several years of college and some previous childcare experience and transform them into first-class nannies.

Contact the American Council of Nanny Schools for the location of the closest schools in your area: American Council of Nanny Schools, Delta College, University Center, MI 48710 (517) 686-9000.

Miscellaneous Approaches

In addition to the areas that have been covered, you can get creative and try some of the following techniques:

- Go to your local grocery store. Occasionally there are bulletin boards in the entrance to the grocery store where you can post an advertisement for a housekeeper.

- Offer your home as a "day care site" for two or three children. Run an advertisement in the paper suggesting that your home is available for other children and hire a sitter to take care of your child and these other children. [Make sure that you check the state and local ordinances about running a day care facility, however, because you do not want to have so many children at your home that you are governed by these regulations.] If you do it this way, you will be charging the other parents for the care of their children and will ultimately have provided a housekeeper for your family at no cost at all.

- Go to a local park where youngsters and their housekeepers are frequently found on a sunny afternoon. Sit down on a bench and start talking to some of these other housekeepers, and you may find an unhappy one in the group. If you leave your name and telephone number, they may contact you when they are interested in changing jobs.

- Contact the nearest senior citizens recreational center. Many active, vibrant "grandmas" and "grandpas" would love the chance to take care of a child. This source is especially good for the working parent with a part-time job. Housekeeping is usually not an option with this resource.

- Contact the local churches and synagogues and see if the priests, ministers or rabbis know of any women in their congregation who want to take care of children.

Use Of The Agencies

As I said earlier in this chapter, an agency is a quick solution to finding capable childcare. To begin working with an agency, you need to know which agencies are located in your area. To do so, you can check the yellow pages of your telephone directory, or the advertisements in the local newspapers on a Sunday. Many employment agencies run block ads in the Sunday paper and in those advertisements, they identify the people who come to them looking for jobs. The "buzz" words you will be looking for are Housekeepers, Nannies, Governesses, or Childcare Monitors. Make a list of all the agencies in your area and their phone numbers, and keep the list both at home and in your roledex at the office. You never can tell when it will be necessary to contact one of these agencies to answer a question or to help a friend find quality childcare.

When you call the agencies, it is important to have a detailed list of the needed qualifications in front of you as you speak to a representative of each agency.

You will quickly learn that representatives of employment agencies who are responsible for finding work for housekeepers and nannies are bearers of "doom and gloom" information about the availability of these people. The first thing that you will find out is that after you have gone through your carefully prepared checklist of qualifications, the person on the other end of the telephone is going to tell you that you will never find anybody who will do all the things that you have just so carefully explained to them. In addition, no matter what you say you are willing to pay, the person on the other end of the phone is going to tell you that it is not going to be enough to get somebody who could do the things that you just described. So, to deal effectively with agencies that find positions for housekeepers and nannies, you must concentrate on the duties that you want performed by the housekeeper, rather than the money aspect, when negotiating with the representative of the agency. In other words, tell the person on the other end of the phone that money is not going to be a problem and that you are flexible, and let the agencies line up candidates that are appropriate in terms of the responsibilities and duties that must be performed. Then, make your best financial deal with the prospective employee.

I find that it is a much faster process to place your order for childcare in at least two, and preferably more, agencies in your local area. The benefit of doing this is that you get a larger pool of candidates from which to choose. The only drawback might be that you have too many people to see and you will have to be more definitive in pre-selecting who you want to actually spend the time interviewing. Don't make it a habit of telling an agency that you are working with other agencies. They may not be as responsive to you, if they feel that there is too much competition.

Unless you are prepared to hire a nanny to start working within two weeks, you should not begin the search process yet.

Many first-time employers, especially first-time parents-to-be, think they must start the search three to six months prior to the date they anticipate the nanny will start. Then, when they find the right person, they think this person will wait until this magic date in the future. Well, don't count on it!

Housekeepers and nannies generally do not give significant notice to their current employers. If you are interviewing them, they are "hungry" to make the change immediately.

Therefore, you should begin the process approximately six weeks prior to the anticipated start date if you are using resources other than employment agencies. If you use agencies, you should not need more than four weeks lead time.

Use the **"Job Requirements Checklist"** on the next page to assist you in discussing your needs. The answers you provided on the **"Family Fact Sheet"** should be used to complete this checklist.

Job Requirements Checklist

	YES	NO
LIVE-OUT	☐	☐
DRIVER'S LICENSE	☐	☐
LIVE-IN	☐	☐
NON-SMOKER	☐	☐
SPEAK SECOND LANGUAGE	☐	☐
COOK (CHILDREN)	☐	☐
COOK (FAMILY)	☐	☐
LAUNDRY (CHILDREN'S)	☐	☐
LAUNDRY (FAMILY)	☐	☐
GROCERY SHOPPING	☐	☐
VACUUM	☐	☐
DUST	☐	☐
MAKE BEDS	☐	☐
CLEAN BATHROOMS	☐	☐
CLEAN KITCHEN	☐	☐
WASH DISHES	☐	☐
TAKE CARE OF PETS	☐	☐

Chapter III
How to **Pre-Screen** Your Findings

"Family Fact Sheet", keep pre-screening. *You will find the right person for your family.*

Pre-Screening Telephone Interview Questionnaire

DATE: _____

CANDIDATE'S NAME: _____

TELEPHONE NUMBER: _____

- -

1. Why are you interested in the position?

2. Where are you working now?

3. How long have you been working there?

4. How many child(ren) are you taking care of? How old and what sex?

5. Where do you live?

6. How would you commute to the job? How long will it take you to make the trip?

7. If you are responsible for taking care of anyone in your home, children or parents, how will you handle the responsibility for their care while you are at work?

8. The job involves some overtime with little advance notice. How would you handle that?

9. Are you able to give references that can be checked in advance of an interview?

10. Can you cook? (iron, drive etc.)

11. Do you smoke?

12. What are you looking for in terms of salary?

13. When are you available to begin work?

Invited For Interview   ☐ Yes   ☐ No

Date: _____ Time: _____

Location: _____

Chapter IV

How to **Interview** The Candidates

HOW TO INTERVIEW THE CANDIDATES

Well, you have *almost* picked the perfect nanny. You have thought through and documented your needs. You have explained these needs and requirements to an agency representative, or in a newspaper advertisement, or on a bulletin board, or through other methods described in Chapter Two. You have pre-screened the applicants over the telephone. You have invited the best candidates for a personal interview.

Now what??? Now, you are in the home stretch. Use Part A of the **"Interview Questionnaire"** which follows to help you ask the right questions during the interview. Make sure you note the time of arrival for each candidate and bring your child(ren) into the room to see how the candidate interacts with him/her/them.

Here are some points worth noting:

● Beware of candidates who are late for the interview. It could signify the start of a chronic lateness problem.

● Be up front about your policies on vacation and sick days. My policies go something like this:

Vacation: During the first year of employment, I recommend a one-week vacation, to be taken at the time *you* specify. Some of my friends prefer to coincide the nanny's vacation with their own vacation because they plan to travel with their children. Other friends choose the opposite approach, and go away without the children for a bit of rest and relaxation. The nanny, therefore, would not be scheduled for vacation that week. Either way, the nanny should know up front how you are going to treat her/his vacation.

If you plan to vacation away from home with your child(ren) for a period longer than one week and do not intend to take the nanny with you, you should still pay her/his salary. Just because you are not there does not mean the nanny should not be compensated.

Sick Days: How many sick days in one year are considered reasonable? I am asked that question more frequently than any other one, and I do not have a definitive answer. It depends upon how much you, as an employer, are willing to tolerate. Remember, you will be the one scrambling to find a substitute at the last minute every time a sick day is taken.

So, clearly state your policy during the interview in hopes that you can entice the "slightly under the weather" nanny to come to work when an illness is very mild.

I recommend that you agree to pay for three sick days the first year. Additional sick days go unpaid. As an enticement to avoid even those three days, tell the nanny that you will pay her/him double for the days, if they are not taken.

- Be aware of your legal responsibilities and discuss these responsibilities with the prospective employee during the interview. Briefly, you must understand and be able to explain the effects of withholding Social Security Tax and Federal Income Tax from the agreed-upon salary. *Do not wait until the first payday to explain the finances.* Misunderstandings concerning money are almost always disastrous.

Upon completion of the interview, *immediately* complete Part B of the questionnaire, "RATING SCALE."

Candidates who score a majority of "Outstandings" should be considered for job offers, subject, of course, to a thorough reference check. Candidates with any "Below Average" scores should be eliminated.

Tell all interviewed candidates that you will call them and advise them of their status. Call those who "bombed out" the same day and tell them that you have picked someone else. For the ones that you are seriously considering, you must allow yourself enough time to check references thoroughly and to feel comfortable with your decision.

Interview Questionnaire

PART A

PERSONAL DATA

Name: _____ Date: _____

Time of Interview: _____

Home Address: _____

Home Telephone Number: _____

EMPLOYMENT HISTORY [Go Back Five Years]

Current Employer: _____

Address: _____

Telephone Number: _____

Age and Sex of Child(ren): _____

Live-in or Live-out: _____

Reason For Leaving: _____

Previous Employer: _____

Address: _____

Telephone Number: _____

Age and Sex of Child(ren): _____

Live-in or Live-out: _____

Reason For Leaving: _____

How Many Work Days Have You Lost Due to Illness in the
Past Year? _____

What Was the Nature of the Illness(es): _____

Can You Operate a	Yes	No
Washing Machine	☐	☐
Dryer	☐	☐
Vacuum Cleaner	☐	☐
Microwave Oven	☐	☐
Do You Iron?	☐	☐

Do You Cook? Simple ☐   Gourmet ☐

	Yes	No
Do You Know How To Drive?	☐	☐
Do You Have a Valid Driver's License?	☐	☐
Do You Have Any Physical Limitations or Health Problems That Could Hinder Your Job Performance?	☐	☐
Have You Ever Been Convicted of a Crime?	☐	☐

PART B

RATING SCALE

	Outstanding	Average	Below Average
1. On Time For Interview	Early	On Time	Late
2. Well Groomed	☐	☐	☐
3. Articulate	☐	☐	☐
4. Seems Interested in Position	☐	☐	☐

5. Seems Interested in
   Child(ren) ☐ ☐ ☐

6. Child(ren) Seem
   Interested in Her/Him ☐ ☐ ☐

7. Good Command of
   English
   (Or Relevant Language) ☐ ☐ ☐

8. Felt Comfortable Talking
   to Her/Him ☐ ☐ ☐

9. Seems Trustworthy ☐ ☐ ☐

10. Notes

	Yes	No
11. Should Consider For Offer	☐	☐

Chapter V
How to **Interview** The References

HOW TO INTERVIEW THE REFERENCES

A thorough phone interview of *all* the references provided by your leading job contenders is as important as the applicant's interview.

Stay clear of the candidate who has lied about previous employment or who has major unexplained gaps in employment over the last five years. Also, beware of the applicant with a previous attendance or lateness problem.

Try to draw the speaker out and learn as much as you can about the family your potential nanny worked for last.

- Does the number and/or ages of the child(ren) in her/his last place of employment have any resemblance to your family?

- Does the reference sound trustworthy?

- If the applicant was fired, does the candidate's version of the incident coincide with the reference's version of the incident? By the way, if the candidate was fired, it is not always a reason to avoid hiring her/him. For example, if an applicant for a live-in position was asked to work 3 weeks straight without a day off and then was fired for not performing the job in an enthusiastic way, the situation is understandable.

Use the **"Reference Questionnaire"** below when speaking to your applicant's previous employers.

Reference Questionnaire

CANDIDATE'S NAME: _____

REFERENCE'S NAME: _____

----

1. List her/his major responsibilities.

2. What were her/his strengths?

3. What were her/his weaknesses?

4. What did you think of her/his overall performance?

5. What were her/his hours?

6. Was she/he on time for work (live-out)?

7. Did she/he stay late if you needed her/him to?

8. Did she/he have any personal family obligations which resulted in time away from the job?

9. How much time did she/he lose because of illness?

10. How much did you pay her/him? (You may not get an answer to this question.)

11. Why is she/he no longer working for you?

12. Would you rehire her/him? (should only be asked if nanny resigned)

Chapter VI
How to Make the **Final Pick**

HOW TO MAKE THE FINAL PICK

If you have followed the guidelines in the first five chapters, the final pick is the easiest part of the process.

Take the candidate whose scores on the rating scale, when coupled with the feedback from the references, appears to be the best. That combination should give your family a "winner" who satisfies the majority of your needs.

Included below is a checklist to help your new nanny get acclimated to your family. By outlining the basics in an easy to follow weekly chart, the first few weeks together will go more smoothly.

Nanny's Weekly Checklist

	Monday	Tuesday	Wednesday	Thursday	Friday
Carpool					
Vacuum					
Clean Bathrooms					
Clean Kitchen					
Make Beds					
Change Beds					
Dust					
Iron					
Make Dinner					
Laundry					
Grocery Shopping					

Important Telephone Numbers

Your Home No.

Your Office No.

Spouse's Office No.

Doctor

Fire Dept.

Nanny's Home No.

Secretary's Name

Secretary's Name

Police Dept.

Child's School

Chapter VII
What To Do For A "Quick Fix"

WHAT TO DO FOR A "QUICK FIX"

By now, you have a perfect nanny selected for your family. But even perfect nannies get sick or have emergencies which means *you* need to have a contingency plan ready for implementation.

My contingency plan goes something like this:

1. Keep a list of nurses registries and employment agencies specializing in same day service next to the home and office phones. A nurse, preferably a licensed practical rather than a registered nurse, is expensive but can be worth it for the peace of mind.

2. Keep a list of all local parents with nannies or housekeepers. I have established a "reciprocal emergency" agreement which is only used in a real bind. You drop your child off at the house with the working housekeeper.

3. Call a relative. Sometimes a relative who hasn't seen your child(ren) in a while will "pitch in" in a pinch.

4. Split the workday with your spouse. Obviously, this only works if you have a spouse to share with. One parent goes into work early and goes home at lunchtime to relieve the other parent who can then work late.

5. Bring your child to work. This only works if you have an understanding boss.

6. Stay home and take a vacation day. This is the "if everything else fails" approach. Besides, you probably could use a break!!

Supplemental Forms

Job Requirements Checklist

	YES	NO
LIVE-OUT	☐	☐
DRIVER'S LICENSE	☐	☐
LIVE-IN	☐	☐
NON-SMOKER	☐	☐
SPEAK SECOND LANGUAGE	☐	☐
COOK (CHILDREN)	☐	☐
COOK (FAMILY)	☐	☐
LAUNDRY (CHILDREN'S)	☐	☐
LAUNDRY (FAMILY)	☐	☐
GROCERY SHOPPING	☐	☐
VACUUM	☐	☐
DUST	☐	☐
MAKE BEDS	☐	☐
CLEAN BATHROOMS	☐	☐
CLEAN KITCHEN	☐	☐
WASH DISHES	☐	☐
TAKE CARE OF PETS	☐	☐

Job Requirements Checklist

	YES	NO
LIVE-OUT	☐	☐
DRIVER'S LICENSE	☐	☐
LIVE-IN	☐	☐
NON-SMOKER	☐	☐
SPEAK SECOND LANGUAGE	☐	☐
COOK (CHILDREN)	☐	☐
COOK (FAMILY)	☐	☐
LAUNDRY (CHILDREN'S)	☐	☐
LAUNDRY (FAMILY)	☐	☐
GROCERY SHOPPING	☐	☐
VACUUM	☐	☐
DUST	☐	☐
MAKE BEDS	☐	☐
CLEAN BATHROOMS	☐	☐
CLEAN KITCHEN	☐	☐
WASH DISHES	☐	☐
TAKE CARE OF PETS	☐	☐

Job Requirements Checklist

	YES	NO
LIVE-OUT	☐	☐
DRIVER'S LICENSE	☐	☐
LIVE-IN	☐	☐
NON-SMOKER	☐	☐
SPEAK SECOND LANGUAGE	☐	☐
COOK (CHILDREN)	☐	☐
COOK (FAMILY)	☐	☐
LAUNDRY (CHILDREN'S)	☐	☐
LAUNDRY (FAMILY)	☐	☐
GROCERY SHOPPING	☐	☐
VACUUM	☐	☐
DUST	☐	☐
MAKE BEDS	☐	☐
CLEAN BATHROOMS	☐	☐
CLEAN KITCHEN	☐	☐
WASH DISHES	☐	☐
TAKE CARE OF PETS	☐	☐

Job Requirements Checklist

	YES	NO
LIVE-OUT	☐	☐
DRIVER'S LICENSE	☐	☐
LIVE-IN	☐	☐
NON-SMOKER	☐	☐
SPEAK SECOND LANGUAGE	☐	☐
COOK (CHILDREN)	☐	☐
COOK (FAMILY)	☐	☐
LAUNDRY (CHILDREN'S)	☐	☐
LAUNDRY (FAMILY)	☐	☐
GROCERY SHOPPING	☐	☐
VACUUM	☐	☐
DUST	☐	☐
MAKE BEDS	☐	☐
CLEAN BATHROOMS	☐	☐
CLEAN KITCHEN	☐	☐
WASH DISHES	☐	☐
TAKE CARE OF PETS	☐	☐

Pre-Screening Telephone Interview Questionnaire

DATE: _____

CANDIDATE'S NAME: _____

TELEPHONE NUMBER: _____

1. Why are you interested in the position?

2. Where are you working now?

3. How long have you been working there?

4. How many child(ren) are your taking care of? How old and what sex?

5. Where do you live?

6. How would you commute to the job? How long will it take you to make the trip?

7. The job involves some overtime with little advance notice. How would you handle that?

8. Are you able to give references that can be checked in advance of an interview?

9. Can you cook? (iron, drive etc.)

10. Do you smoke?

11. What are you looking for in terms of salary?

12. When are you available to begin work?

Invited For Interview   ☐ Yes   ☐ No

Date: _____ Time: _____

Location: _____

Pre-Screening Telephone Interview Questionnaire

DATE: _____

CANDIDATE'S NAME: _____

TELEPHONE NUMBER: _____

....

1. Why are you interested in the position?

2. Where are you working now?

3. How long have you been working there?

4. How many child(ren) are your taking care of? How old and what sex?

5. Where do you live?

6. How would you commute to the job? How long will it take you to make the trip?

7. The job involves some overtime with little advance notice. How would you handle that?

8. Are you able to give references that can be checked in advance of an interview?

9. Can you cook? (iron, drive etc.)

10. Do you smoke?

11. What are you looking for in terms of salary?

12. When are you available to begin work?

Invited For Interview   ☐ Yes   ☐ No

Date: _____ Time: _____

Location: _____

Pre-Screening Telephone Interview Questionnaire

DATE: _____

CANDIDATE'S NAME: _____

TELEPHONE NUMBER: _____

1. Why are you interested in the position?

2. Where are you working now?

3. How long have you been working there?

4. How many child(ren) are your taking care of? How old and what sex?

5. Where do you live?

6. How would you commute to the job? How long will it take you to make the trip?

7. The job involves some overtime with little advance notice. How would you handle that?

8. Are you able to give references that can be checked in advance of an interview?

9. Can you cook? (iron, drive etc.)

10. Do you smoke?

11. What are you looking for in terms of salary?

12. When are you available to begin work?

Invited For Interview ☐ Yes ☐ No

Date: _____ Time: _____

Location: _____

Pre-Screening Telephone Interview Questionnaire

DATE: _____

CANDIDATE'S NAME: _____

TELEPHONE NUMBER: _____

....

1. Why are you interested in the position?

2. Where are you working now?

3. How long have you been working there?

4. How many child(ren) are your taking care of? How old and what sex?

5. Where do you live?

6. How would you commute to the job? How long will it take you to make the trip?

7. The job involves some overtime with little advance notice. How would you handle that?

8. Are you able to give references that can be checked in advance of an interview?

9. Can you cook? (iron, drive etc.)

10. Do you smoke?

11. What are you looking for in terms of salary?

12. When are you available to begin work?

Invited For Interview   ☐ Yes   ☐ No

Date: _____ Time: _____

Location: _____

Interview Questionnaire

PART A

PERSONAL DATA

Name: _____ Date: _____

Time of Interview: _____

Home Address: _____

Home Telephone Number: _____

EMPLOYMENT HISTORY [Go Back Five Years]

Current Employer: _____

Address: _____

Telephone Number: _____

Age and Sex of Child(ren): _____

Live-in or Live-out: _____

Reason For Leaving: _____

Previous Employer: _____

Address: _____

Telephone Number: _____

Age and Sex of Child(ren): _____

Live-in or Live-out: _____

Reason For Leaving: _____

How Many Work Days Have You Lost Due to Illness in the

Past Year? _____

What Was the Nature of the Illness(es): _____

Can You Operate a	Yes	No
Washing Machine	☐	☐
Dryer	☐	☐
Vacuum Cleaner	☐	☐
Microwave Oven	☐	☐
Do You Iron?	☐	☐

Do You Cook? Simple ☐   Gourmet ☐

	Yes	No
Do You Know How To Drive?	☐	☐
Do You Have a Valid Driver's License?	☐	☐
Do You Have Any Physical Limitations or Health Problems That Could Hinder Your Job Performance?	☐	☐
Have You Ever Been Convicted of a Crime?	☐	☐

PART B

RATING SCALE

	Outstanding	Average	Below Average
1. On Time For Interview	Early	On Time	Late
2. Well Groomed	☐	☐	☐
3. Articulate	☐	☐	☐
4. Seems Interested in Position	☐	☐	☐
5. Seems Interested in Child(ren)	☐	☐	☐
6. Child(ren) Seem Interested in Her/Him	☐	☐	☐

	Outstanding	Average	Below Average
RATING SCALE			

RATING SCALE

7. Good Command of
    English
    (Or Relevant Language)   ☐   ☐   ☐

8. Felt Comfortable Talking
    to Her/Him   ☐   ☐   ☐

9. Seems Trustworthy   ☐   ☐   ☐

10. Notes

	Yes	No
11. Should Consider For Offer	☐	☐

Interview Questionnaire

PART A

PERSONAL DATA

Name: _____ Date: _____

Time of Interview: _____

Home Address: _____

Home Telephone Number: _____

EMPLOYMENT HISTORY [Go Back Five Years]

Current Employer: _____

Address: _____

Telephone Number: _____

Age and Sex of Child(ren): _____

Live-in or Live-out: _____

Reason For Leaving: _____

Previous Employer: _____

Address: _____

Telephone Number: _____

Age and Sex of Child(ren): _____

Live-in or Live-out: _____

Reason For Leaving: _____

How Many Work Days Have You Lost Due to Illness in the

Past Year? _____

What Was the Nature of the Illness(es): _____

Can You Operate a	Yes	No
Washing Machine	☐	☐
Dryer	☐	☐
Vacuum Cleaner	☐	☐
Microwave Oven	☐	☐
Do You Iron?	☐	☐
Do You Cook? Simple ☐ Gourmet ☐		
Do You Know How To Drive?	☐	☐
Do You Have a Valid Driver's License?	☐	☐
Do You Have Any Physical Limitations or Health Problems That Could Hinder Your Job Performance?	☐	☐
Have You Ever Been Convicted of a Crime?	☐	☐

PART B

RATING SCALE	Outstanding	Average	Below Average
1. On Time For Interview	Early	On Time	Late
2. Well Groomed	☐	☐	☐
3. Articulate	☐	☐	☐
4. Seems Interested in Position	☐	☐	☐
5. Seems Interested in Child(ren)	☐	☐	☐
6. Child(ren) Seem Interested in Her/Him	☐	☐	☐

RATING SCALE   <u>**Outstanding**</u> <u>**Average**</u> <u>**Below Average**</u>

7. Good Command of
   English
   (Or Relevant Language)   ☐   ☐   ☐

8. Felt Comfortable Talking
   to Her/Him   ☐   ☐   ☐

9. Seems Trustworthy   ☐   ☐   ☐

10. Notes

                                    Yes   No
11. Should Consider For Offer   ☐   ☐

Interview Questionnaire

PART A

PERSONAL DATA

Name: _____ Date: _____

Time of Interview: _____

Home Address: _____

Home Telephone Number: _____

EMPLOYMENT HISTORY [Go Back Five Years]

Current Employer: _____

Address: _____

Telephone Number: _____

Age and Sex of Child(ren): _____

Live-in or Live-out: _____

Reason For Leaving: _____

Previous Employer: _____

Address: _____

Telephone Number: _____

Age and Sex of Child(ren): _____

Live-in or Live-out: _____

Reason For Leaving: _____

How Many Work Days Have You Lost Due to Illness in the

Past Year? _____

What Was the Nature of the Illness(es): _____

Can You Operate a	Yes	No
Washing Machine	☐	☐
Dryer	☐	☐
Vacuum Cleaner	☐	☐
Microwave Oven	☐	☐
Do You Iron?	☐	☐
Do You Cook? Simple ☐ Gourmet ☐		
Do You Know How To Drive?	☐	☐
Do You Have a Valid Driver's License?	☐	☐
Do You Have Any Physical Limitations or Health Problems That Could Hinder Your Job Performance?	☐	☐
Have You Ever Been Convicted of a Crime?	☐	☐

PART B

RATING SCALE

	Outstanding	Average	Below Average
1. On Time For Interview	Early	On Time	Late
2. Well Groomed	☐	☐	☐
3. Articulate	☐	☐	☐
4. Seems Interested in Position	☐	☐	☐
5. Seems Interested in Child(ren)	☐	☐	☐
6. Child(ren) Seem Interested in Her/Him	☐	☐	☐

RATING SCALE	Outstanding	Average	Below Average
7. Good Command of English (Or Relevant Language)	☐	☐	☐
8. Felt Comfortable Talking to Her/Him	☐	☐	☐
9. Seems Trustworthy	☐	☐	☐

10. Notes

	Yes	No
11. Should Consider For Offer	☐	☐

Interview Questionnaire

PART A

PERSONAL DATA

Name: _____ Date: _____

Time of Interview: _____

Home Address: _____

Home Telephone Number: _____

EMPLOYMENT HISTORY [Go Back Five Years]

Current Employer: _____

Address: _____

Telephone Number: _____

Age and Sex of Child(ren): _____

Live-in or Live-out: _____

Reason For Leaving: _____

Previous Employer: _____

Address: _____

Telephone Number: _____

Age and Sex of Child(ren): _____

Live-in or Live-out: _____

Reason For Leaving: _____

How Many Work Days Have You Lost Due to Illness in the

Past Year? _____

What Was the Nature of the Illness(es): _____

Can You Operate a	Yes	No
Washing Machine	☐	☐
Dryer	☐	☐
Vacuum Cleaner	☐	☐
Microwave Oven	☐	☐
Do You Iron?	☐	☐

Do You Cook? Simple ☐   Gourmet ☐

	Yes	No
Do You Know How To Drive?	☐	☐
Do You Have a Valid Driver's License?	☐	☐
Do You Have Any Physical Limitations or Health Problems That Could Hinder Your Job Performance?	☐	☐
Have You Ever Been Convicted of a Crime?	☐	☐

PART B

RATING SCALE

	Outstanding	Average	Below Average
1. On Time For Interview	Early	On Time	Late
2. Well Groomed	☐	☐	☐
3. Articulate	☐	☐	☐
4. Seems Interested in Position	☐	☐	☐
5. Seems Interested in Child(ren)	☐	☐	☐
6. Child(ren) Seem Interested in Her/Him	☐	☐	☐

RATING SCALE

	Outstanding	Average	Below Average
7. Good Command of English (Or Relevant Language)	☐	☐	☐
8. Felt Comfortable Talking to Her/Him	☐	☐	☐
9. Seems Trustworthy	☐	☐	☐

10. Notes

	Yes	No
11. Should Consider For Offer	☐	☐

Reference Questionnaire

CANDIDATE'S NAME:_____

REFERENCE'S NAME:_____

----

1. List her/his major responsibilities.

2. What were her/his strengths?

3. What were her/his weakness?

4. What did you think of her/his overall performance?

5. What were her/his hours?

6. Was she/he on time for work (live-out)?

7. Did she/he stay late if you needed her/him to?

8. How much time did she/he lose because of illness?

9. How much did you pay her/him? (You may not get an answer to this question.)

10. Why is she/he no longer working for you?

11. Would you rehire her/him? (should only be asked if nanny resigned)

Reference Questionnaire

CANDIDATE'S NAME:_____

REFERENCE'S NAME:_____

----

1. List her/his major responsibilities.

2. What were her/his strengths?

3. What were her/his weakness?

4. What did you think of her/his overall performance?

5. What were her/his hours?

6. Was she/he on time for work (live-out)?

7. Did she/he stay late if you needed her/him to?

8. How much time did she/he lose because of illness?

9. How much did you pay her/him? (You may not get an answer to this question.)

10. Why is she/he no longer working for you?

11. Would you rehire her/him? (should only be asked if nanny resigned)

Reference Questionnaire

CANDIDATE'S NAME:_____

REFERENCE'S NAME:_____

----

1. List her/his major responsibilities.

2. What were her/his strengths?

3. What were her/his weakness?

4. What did you think of her/his overall performance?

5. What were her/his hours?

6. Was she/he on time for work (live-out)?

7. Did she/he stay late if you needed her/him to?

8. How much time did she/he lose because of illness?

9. How much did you pay her/him? (You may not get an answer to this question.)

10. Why is she/he no longer working for you?

11. Would you rehire her/him? (should only be asked if nanny resigned)

Reference Questionnaire

CANDIDATE'S NAME:_____

REFERENCE'S NAME:_____

---

1. List her/his major responsibilities.

2. What were her/his strengths?

3. What were her/his weakness?

4. What did you think of her/his overall performance?

5. What were her/his hours?

6. Was she/he on time for work (live-out)?

7. Did she/he stay late if you needed her/him to?

8. How much time did she/he lose because of illness?

9. How much did you pay her/him? (You may not get an answer to this question.)

10. Why is she/he no longer working for you?

11. Would you rehire her/him? (should only be asked if nanny resigned)

Nanny's Weekly Checklist

	Monday	Tuesday	Wednesday	Thursday	Friday
Carpool					
Vacuum					
Clean Bathrooms					
Clean Kitchen					
Make Beds					
Change Beds					
Dust					
Iron					
Make Dinner					
Laundry					
Grocery Shopping					

Important Telephone Numbers

Your Home No.

Your Office No.

Spouse's Office No.

Doctor

Fire Dept.

Nanny's Home No.

Secretary's Name

Secretary's Name

Police Dept.

Child's School

Nanny's Weekly Checklist

	Monday	Tuesday	Wednesday	Thursday	Friday
Carpool					
Vacuum					
Clean Bathrooms					
Clean Kitchen					
Make Beds					
Change Beds					
Dust					
Iron					
Make Dinner					
Laundry					
Grocery Shopping					

Important Telephone Numbers

Your Home No.

Your Office No.

Spouse's Office No.

Doctor

Fire Dept.

Nanny's Home No.

Secretary's Name

Secretary's Name

Police Dept.

Child's School

Nanny's Weekly Checklist

	Monday	Tuesday	Wednesday	Thursday	Friday
Carpool					
Vacuum					
Clean Bathrooms					
Clean Kitchen					
Make Beds					
Change Beds					
Dust					
Iron					
Make Dinner					
Laundry					
Grocery Shopping					

Important Telephone Numbers

Your Home No.

Your Office No.

Spouse's Office No.

Doctor

Fire Dept.

Nanny's Home No.

Secretary's Name

Secretary's Name

Police Dept.

Child's School

Nanny's Weekly Checklist

	Monday	Tuesday	Wednesday	Thursday	Friday
Carpool					
Vacuum					
Clean Bathrooms					
Clean Kitchen					
Make Beds					
Change Beds					
Dust					
Iron					
Make Dinner					
Laundry					
Grocery Shopping					

Important Telephone Numbers

Your Home No.

Your Office No.

Spouse's Office No.

Doctor

Fire Dept.

Nanny's Home No.

Secretary's Name

Secretary's Name

Police Dept.

Child's School

Notes

Notes

Notes

Notes